KESSAI FIXES CREDIT!
(THE ULTIMATE GUIDE TO CREDIT RESTORATION)

By: **Dre Mudaris**
Illustrator By: **Cameron Wilson**

ISBN: 9798510914511

Copyright © 2020 Children To Wealth

All rights reserved.

KESSAI FIXES CREDIT
THE ULTIMATE GUIDE TO CREDIT RESTORATION

All rights reserved.

Reading Levels

Interest Level: K-Gr. 7   DRA Level: 24   Lexile Measure: 770L

Grade Equivalent: 3.7   Guided Reading: M

WATCH ALONG
(SCAN CODE BELOW)

Kessai is with his Mother and Father at a Local First Time Home Buyers Seminar in the community.

Uncle Dre is on stage ending his speech on the benefits of Home Ownership.

"Thank you all for coming out, and I am so excited that you guys are taking steps to become a Homeowner. I want to conclude and leave you all with the 7 Major benefits of home ownership. "Uncle Dre Says.

"Homeownership builds wealth over time; secondly, you build equity each month. Thirdly, you reap mortgage tax deduction benefits. Number four; there are also tax deductions on home equity lines. Number Five is you get capital gains exclusions. Number 6 is that a mortgage is similar to a forced savings plan. Lastly, number seven is long-term buying is cheaper than renting."

The Crowd stands and begins applauding as Uncle Dre exits the stage.

Equity- Ownership interest in a firm. Also, the residual dollar value of a futures trading account, assuming its liquidation is at the going trade price. In real estate, dollar difference between what a property could be sold for and debts claimed against it. In a brokerage account, equity equals the value of the account's securities minus any debit balance in a margin account. Equity is also shorthand for stock market investments.

Tax Deduction- A tax deduction is a deduction that lowers a person's tax liability by lowering their taxable income. Deductions are typically expenses that the taxpayer incurs during the year that can be applied against or subtracted from their gross income in order to figure out how much tax is owed.

Mortgage- A mortgage is a debt instrument, secured by the collateral of specified real estate property, that the borrower is obliged to pay back with a predetermined set of payments.

Home Equity Line- Is a revolving source of funds, much like a credit card, that you can access as you choose. Most banks offer a number of different ways to access those funds, whether it's through an online transfer, writing a check, or using a credit card connected to your account.

Capital Gain- Profit from the sale of property or an investment.

Kessai notices his father and mother are a little down, while the other parents seem to be motivated after Uncle Dre's Speech.

"What's wrong, pops?" Kessai asks.

"I just really want to get you and your mom into a house," Kessai's dad responds.

"What's stopping us?" Kessai asks.

"It's our credit, son." Kessai's father says, discouraged.

"Oh, that's not an issue pops. My best friend Jasiah is the nephew of Uncle Dre; I'll text him to see if he can set up a meeting for us and Uncle Dre to see if he can help." Kessai says.

"Sure, son, that'll be great," Kessai's Dad says.

Next day Kessai runs into the house excited.

"Mommy and daddy guess what! Guess what!" Kessai screams.

"Calm down son, what is it?" Kessai's mom asks.

"I saw Jasiah today in school and he said that Uncle Dre can actually stop by later today. Can we invite him to dinner? Please! Please!"

"Of course son, That's no problem. Tell him to come on over." Kessai's father says.

"Yay!" Kessai says in excitement.

Ding Dong!

"He is here!" Kessai shouts.

Mother and Father open the door and see Uncle Dre with his briefcase.

"Hey, Uncle Dre," Kessai's father says as he greets Uncle Dre.

"You made it!" Kessai says.

"I sure did; I wouldn't miss dinner with you guys for the world," Uncle Dre says.

"Ok, great, 'cause dinner is cooked," Kessai's mom says.

They proceed to walk to the dinner table.

"Before we bless the food and eat, I want to go over some things with you from the first time Home buyer seminar that I saw you guys at," Uncle Dre says.

"Sure, what did you have in mind," Kessai's Father asks.

"Well, I want to dive deeper and discuss how I can help you boost your credit. I like to have my clients in the best credit situation when starting their journey to home ownership."

"But how did you know." Kessai's father says..

"Know what?" Uncle Dre says confused.

"Oh nothing, continue." Kessai's dad says as he and Kessai look at each other confused on how Uncle Dre knew why he was there.

"Ok great, first thing first. We would need to evaluate your credit situation. My coaching services are specifically intended for families who are looking to establish credit, re-establish credit or get a good boost on their credit score on their current credit report." Uncle Dre says.

"Sounds like we are your family, how do we begin." Kessai's Father says.

"Well, first we will need to find out which category you guys fit in to, in terms of the accounts we will target. The type of categories consist of; TAX LIENS ANY TYPE OF COLLECTION ACCOUNTS, DELINQUENT PUBLIC RECORDS, DEFAULTED STUDENT LOANS, REPOSSESIONS, FORECLOSURES, and ANY OTHER CLOSED DELINQUENTACCOUNT."

Kessai asks, "What if a family has no credit and they are looking to boost their credit?"

"Kessai, that's a good question," Uncle Dre responds.

"You see, there are two major things you can do to boost your credit fast. Super-fast boost, which is the most popular boost, but it will cost you some money, or the old-fashioned credit boost, which is free but is a little bit more time-consuming."

"I have some savings. Let's go with the super-fast way," Kessai's Mom suggests.

The Kessai Family smiles.

"Ok, sounds good. Let's begin." Uncle Dre says.

"The most popular way, and the way we are going to use, to get your credit score boosted fast is to be added on to someone else's account as an authorized user."

"Just Anyone?" Kessai asks.

"No, not anyone; you cannot simply be added to anyone's credit card account. You have to make sure it's someone with a good credit history. The person should not have high utilization."

"Give us an example of high utilization," Kessai's father asks.

"Their credit utilization must be below 25% and at least one year of on-time good payment history. They cannot have any late payments on their record, which will affect you. This can usually be done with a family member or someone you trust. However, Sometimes it is impossible to find people who meet these qualifications. So some people buy trade lines online," Uncle Dre responds.

Using Trade lines is a well-known secret of credit repair companies, mortgage brokers and real-estate agents. These "Trade lines" can boost your credit score by 100s of points literally overnight. Mortgage brokers and real-estate agents have been using trade lines for decades to help their clients quickly boost their credit scores so that they could qualify for loans and home purchases. There is nothing easier and faster than adding a trade line to your credit report to boost your credit score fast, really fast.

"What exactly is a Trade Line," Kessai asks,"A trade line or trade reference as they may also be called is simply an account on your credit report. Every account, whether it is good or bad is called a trade line or trade reference.

"Think of it like this; When someone opens up a credit card, soon, after they receive it in the mail and start using it, it will show up on their credit report. As they use it and pay it off, the banks let the credit bureaus know that they have been making all of their payments on time. As years pass, the credit card account or trade line becomes aged or seasoned. The more age their trade line has, the better it impacts your credit score. The ideal account to have on your credit report is one that has a high limit, a low balance (25% or less), and at least 1-2 years of history. This credit card account is called a revolving trade line, which has 2 years of seasoning. But there is more to know about trade lines than just this... There are different types and different designation; Primary Trade lines and Authorized User Trade lines."

Primary Trader Lines- are accounts that belong to you. This means you're financially responsible for all debts on this account and you are the "Primary Account Holder."

Authorized User trader Lines- Lines are accounts that belong to others and you have been added as an "Authorized User" to that account. This mean that the primary account holder has financial responsibility on this account, even if it's clear that the charges weremade by the authorized user.

"Well, what about us, who are just re-establishing our credit?" Kessai's mom asks.

"That's very simple; you do this by opening a credit account and building credit profile," Uncle Dre responds.

He continues, "I recommend opening two credit card accounts and one installment account to get started. You must PAY YOUR BILLS ON TIME. You don't want too many accounts because too many inquiries will hurt your credit before it starts. The key is to ensure you keep your credit card utilization under 25% and PAY ON TIME. Remember ONE LATE PAYMENT can backtrack your score 20-50 points or more and put you in a worse position than before getting the credit account."

"One of my co-workers said something about secured credit cards. Do those work as well? Also, what exactly is a secured credit card?" Kessai's Dad asks.

"Great question because most people don't know the difference between secured and unsecured credit cards. A secured card requires a cash collateral deposit that becomes the credit line for that account. For example, if you put $700 in the account, you can charge up to $700. You may be able to add to the deposit to add more credit, or sometimes a bank will reward you for good payment and add to your credit line without requesting additional deposits. To get a secured card, you must have at least $300 in most cases," Uncle Dre responds.

"Interesting, and what about those who already have credit." Kessai's Dad asks.

He continues, "such as credit cards, loans, car notes, home loans etc. I know some people who have either fell behind at some point and can't figure out why their credit score has not gone up."

"Well, It doesn't matter what the case scenario may be. The important facts that I'm about to mention will guide whoever in the direction they need to start getting the perfect credit score. First of all, they must evaluate their credit. The number one thing they are looking for is being current on all accounts. Car notes, credit cards, student loans, mortgages and the list goes on." Uncle Dre responds.

CREDIT SCORE

650

"If you are not current on your bills, your credit score is dramatically affected in a negative way. Under your account it should say current. It should not be 30 to 60 days pass due, but current.

"The next important thing to look for is credit card utilization. You must make sure you are NOT over 25% utilization. An example would be if you have a $1000 credit card limit, please stay under $250 usage. Try your best not to use over $250 of this card. If you do have to use over this amount, make sure you pay it back under 25% before your credit card due date," Uncle Dre says.

He continues, "Another thing I'm noticing is that most people think if they
DO NOT use their card, this is helping them. THIS IS NOT TRUE. When
you get your credit card, PLEASE USE IT. Even for gas, groceries, or simply a night out, please USE YOUR CREDIT CARD. Just make sure you follow the steps I just mentioned."

"My issue is the late payments," Kessai's mom says.

"How do you remove them" She adds.

"If you have missed payments, start paying regularly and stay current. Use online bill pay through your bank to schedule automatic payments for your monthly credit card, utility, rent, mortgage, and other bills. Your payment history greatly affects your
credit score, and missed or late payments are
not easily fixed. But
the longer you pay your bills on time, the more your score will increase." Uncle Dre responds.

"I was told, do not be discouraged if our credit score doesn't improve immediately," Kessai's Dad says.

"Paying off a collection will not remove it from your credit report. It'll still stay on there for seven years. AGAIN DO NOT PAY OFF AN ACCOUNT WITH A COLLECTION AGENCY! You have not gotten your debt at that collection agency, so don't pay it there, and in no way would this improve your credit score if you have not got an agreement from that agency to delete that account upon payment," Uncle Dre responds.

Below is an example of how the credit bureaus will knock your score all the way down from one late payment:

People with a 680 saw their score drop to 530. People with 720 saw a drop down to 525. People with 780 saw their credit scores drop as low as 620.

*The only FREE way to recover from this is to actually get current and pay on time for 6 months and you will see your score increase every month.

"Are there any other methods to remove late payments." Kessai's dad asks.

"Yes, The next method to possibly remove late payments is the Goodwill adjustments way."

A good will adjustment refers to a company removing or changing information on your credit file without legal justification. After trying the phone method the next step is to draft a letter and send it through the mail. Since you are not the phone, the company has more time to mull over whether or not to make the adjustment for you. The letter might end up in the hand of someone with more authority to make these kinds of changes.

"Goodwill letters aren't exclusive to just late payments. You can be creative and write a goodwill letter for any negative information on your file," Uncle Dre adds.

"What about ways to avoid late payments?" Kessai's mom asks.

"Like I tell all families, the best way to avoid it is by automatically setting up payments from your checking account. Another way is simply contacting the credit before becoming late. Ask them if they have any payment deferment programs or what you can do to avoid being hit with a late report on your credit report. For car notes, most banks are willing to put your payment to the end of your loan to avoid the late penalty and late reporting. Most credit card companies are willing to adjust your due date three times a year. But you must make it your business to communicate with your lenders and creditors before the fact and due date."

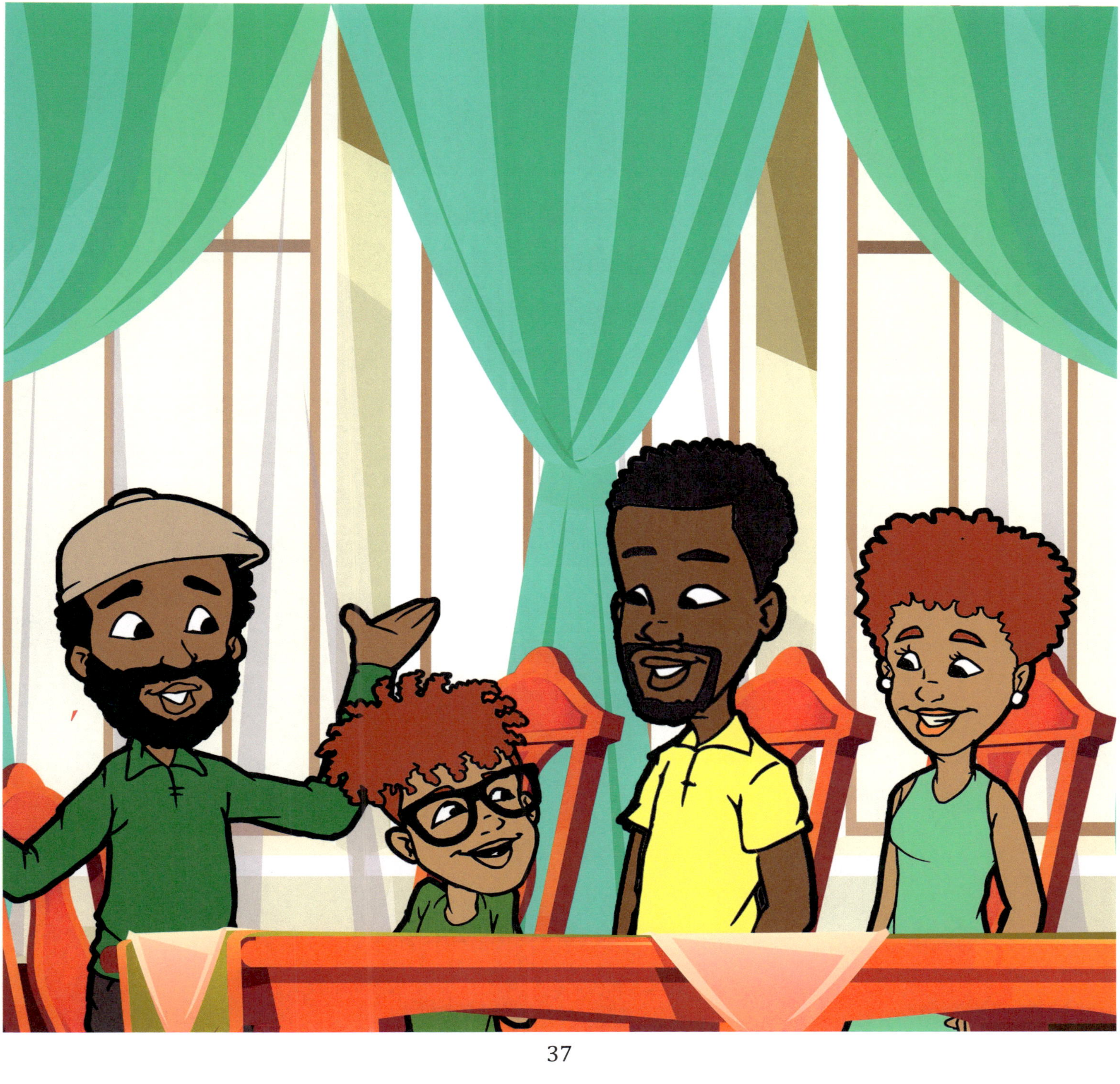

"Even if you have late payments on your report you can always apply for one of the installments accounts or a secured card to simply expand your accounts and credit limit ratio and this will also give you a boost. You can also purchase a trade line to get an immediate boost on your credit even if you have late payments. It will probably be more like a 70 point increase but it will be an immediate credit boost. "Uncle Dre says.

The Kessai family are all taking notes.

Primary Trader Lines are accounts that belong to you. This means you're financially responsible for all debts on this account and you are the Primary Account Holder.

Authorized User Trader Lines are accounts that belong to others and you have been added as an Authorized User to that account. This mean that the primary account holder has financial responsibility on this account, even if it's clear that the charges were made by the authorized user.

Even if you have late payments on your report you can always apply for one of the installments accounts or a secured card to simply expand your accounts and credit limit ratio and this will also give you a boost. You can also purchase a trade line to get an immediate boost on your credit even if you have late payments. It will probably be more like a 70 point increase but it will be an immediate credit boost. Uncle Dre says

The Kessai family are all taking notes.

"Well, that was very helpful," Kessai's father says as he closes up his notebook.

"I don't know about everyone but all of this information worked up an appetite," Kessai's father continues.

"Food is ready,"- Kessai's mom adds.
"That's enough talking for me. Let's Eat!" Uncle Dre Says.

They hold hands as Kessai leads to grace.

The End

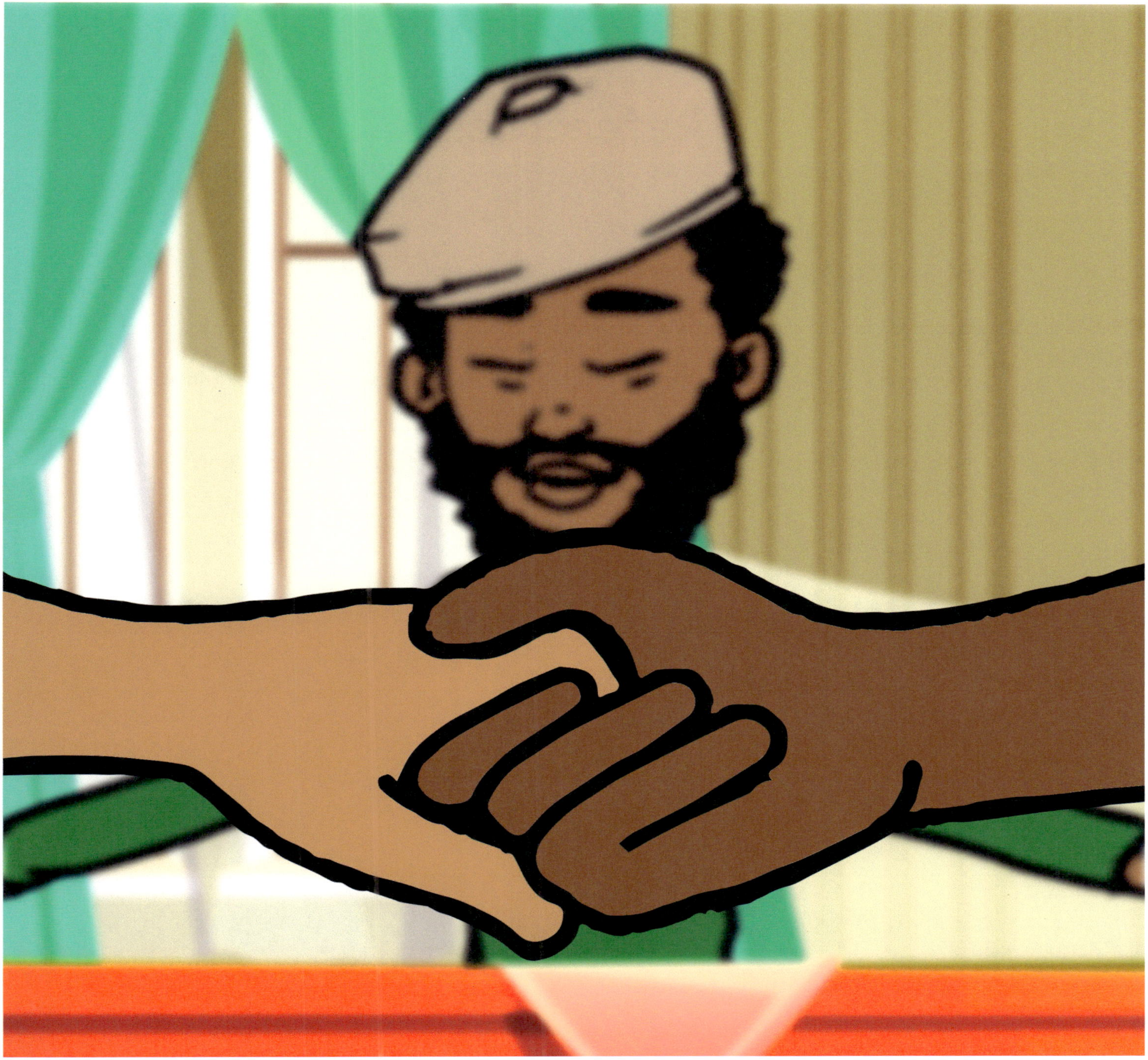

References

Herold, T. (2016): *High Credit Score* .New York City, NY: Public Affairs.

Davenport, A (2018): *Your Score. Mariner Books. Boston*, MA: V

Weaver, B. (2015): *The Easy Section 609 Credit Repair Secret.* New York City, NY: Anchor Books.

Carter, C. (2017): *Keeping Score: What You Need To Know To Make Your Credit Score Grow.* New York City, NY: Lawrence Hill Books.

Terms of Use

All use of the *Kessai Fixes Credit book*, accessible at www.childrentowealth.com and related subdomains (collectively, the "Web site") is subject to the following terms and conditions and our Privacy Policy all of which are deemed a part of and included within these terms and conditions (collectively, the "Terms"). By accessing the book you are acknowledging that you have read, understand, and agree to be bound by these Terms.

These Terms represent a binding contract between you and *Mudaris LLC* (and any of their respective principals, officers, shareholders, members, employees or agents are herein collectively referred to as *"Children To Wealth"* or "we"). These Terms are in addition to any other agreements between you and Mudaris LLC. If you do not agree with any of these terms and conditions, please do not use this book.

Mudaris LLC reserves the right to change, modify, add or remove portions of these Terms at any time for any reason. Such changes shall be effective immediately upon posting. You acknowledge by accessing our book after we have posted changes to this Agreement that you are agreeing to these Terms as modified.

TRADEMARKS, COPYRIGHTS AND OTHER INTELLECTUAL PROPERTY

The content contained in the book is owned, licensed or otherwise lawfully used by *Mudaris LLC* and is protected by applicable copyrights, trademarks, service marks, and/or other intellectual property rights. Mudaris LLC hereby grants you access to its original content pursuant to a Creative Commons Attribution-Noncommercial-ShareAlike License, the terms of which are accessible at: http://creativecommons.org/licenses/by-nc-sa/3.0/legalcode. *Mudaris LLC* hereby expressly reserves all rights not expressly granted in and to the book and its content.

Visit ChildrenToWealth.com and view more books that you will Enjoy!

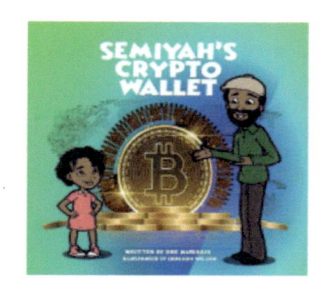

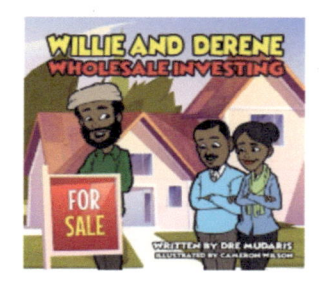

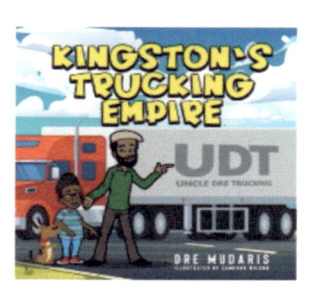

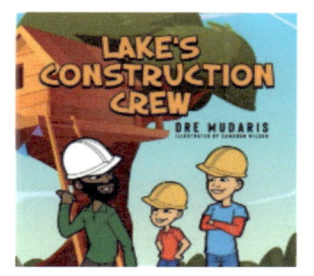

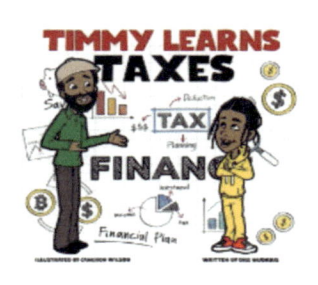

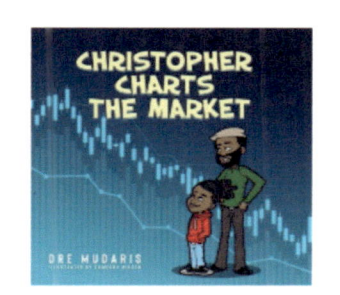

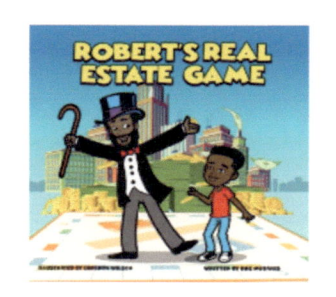

- Semiyah's Crypto Wallet
- Willie and Derene Wholesale Investing
- Kingston's Trucking Empire
- Haylee Explores Her Roots (A Deep Dive Into The Slavery)
- Claire's NFT Collection
- Lake's Construction Crew
- Chase and Noah's STEM Program
- Daveon Makes Sense of Saving Cents
- Timmy Learns Taxes
- Christopher Charts The Market
- Leah's Online Store
- Robert's Real Estate Game

And Much More !!!

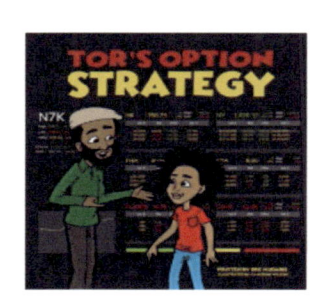

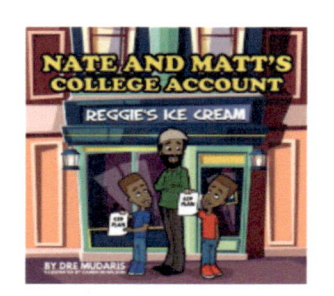

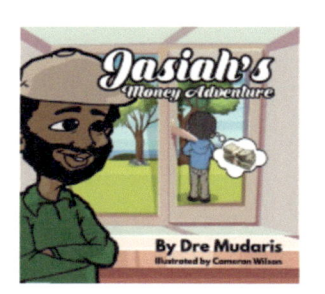

- Tor's Option Strategy
- Mary's Mental Re-Charge
- Nate and Matt's College Account
- Jasiah's Money Adventure

Made in the USA
Columbia, SC
12 August 2024